Stop Procrastinating About Estate Planning

What We Can Learn From Celebrity Mistakes

By

Natalie Johnson

© 2014 All Rights Reserved

Text copyright reserved. Natalie Johnson

The contents of this book may not be reproduced, duplicated or transmitted without direct written permission from the author.

Disclaimer: All attempts have been made by the author to provide factual and accurate content. No responsibility will be taken by the author or publisher for any damages caused by misuse of the contents described in this book. The content of this book has been derived from various sources. Please consult an expert before attempting anything described in this book.

Table of Contents

Introduction	1
Chapter 1. Getting Your Affairs In Order through estate planning	3
What is Estate Planning?	3
Different options available in estate planning	4
Celebrity Mistakes in Estate Planning	11
Chapter 2. Celebrities Who Were Not Able To Write A Will	13
Chapter 3. On Making The Necessary Updates To An Estate Plan	19
Chapter 4. When Estate Taxes Attack the Estate Plan	25
Chapter 5. When Estate Planning Goes Terribly Wrong	39
Chapter 6. When There is An Estate Plan But it Lacks Adequate Planning	44
Chapter 7. Celebrity's Dumb Mistakes in Estate Planning	49
Conclusion	55

Introduction

I want to thank you and congratulate you for downloading the book, **"Stop Procrastinating About Estate Planning: What We Can Learn From Celebrity Mistakes"**.

This book contains proven steps and strategies on how to successfully execute estate planning by learning the different mistakes that celebrities made in their own estate plan. Every case of celebrity mistake discussed in this ebook also carries an important estate planning lesson you can use. Please be mindful that the sooner you make an estate plan, the better. Procrastinating in estate planning should be avoided.

Each chapter of this book focuses on an estate planning error of different celebrities and well-known individuals. There are stories that will teach you about dying without a Will, not updating a Will and naming the appropriate guardian for your children. There is also a chapter that will guide you through estate taxes and probate court.

Besides these, this book has the basics of estate planning and what you need to know about drafting an estate plan efficiently. Feel free to flip the next pages and start securing the financial situation of your loved ones and make things a bit easier for them even after death with estate planning.

Natalie Johnson

Thanks again for downloading this book. I hope you enjoy it!

Chapter 1
Getting Your Affairs In Order through estate planning

Most of the time, people are afraid of the word "death" because it basically means that their physical presence would be no longer available in this world. However, death does not only focus on the emotional side of things, it is also associated with financial aspects particularly assets, properties and other issues. Estate planning can also address wishes of an individual toward the loved ones before he or she dies.

What is Estate Planning?
Estate planning is an important step that anyone can embark on before death or incapacity happens. Preparing for such circumstances involves securing the financial stability of the family. Estate planning also addresses how the estate of deceased would be transferred to the beneficiaries and heirs.

An estate is described as all the property owned by the deceased person. It includes life insurance policies, bank accounts, real estate, stocks, securities and even personal properties such as vehicles, jewelry and artwork.

Everyone has an estate, regardless of their profession, career or financial situation before they died. People who have a vast number of assets and properties are celebrities who earned fame and fortune in the entertainment industry.

Unfortunately, when a person dies, the estate he or she accumulated Will be left behind. These properties can be transferred to the loved ones of the deceased. Transferring the assets and properties of the deceased is not as simple as it may sound. There are a lot of factors to consider because one simple mistake may result in a huge loss.

Different options available in estate planning

Estate planning offers different options. Each option may benefit an individual, depending on the given situation. For example, a Will and testament is the most common way to clarify their wishes in how their estate should be handled upon death. Although Wills are one of the basic estate planning options, it may not be best for everyone. The same goes with Trusts and power of attorney.

Although a Will is the most common option in estate planning, many Americans are not familiar with Wills. In fact, a statistic revealed that 57 percent of American consumers do not have a Will. Sixty-nine percent parents with children do not also have a Will.

Wills

Stop Procrastinating About Estate Planning:

A Will is a legal document that determines who should inherit the estate. People use a Will and testament to express their deepest sentiments to their loved one as well. This document also relieves surviving family from the difficult transition of estate in the event of death.

A Will lists all the estate, the people who will receive the property and wishes to the surviving family. It also provides instructions regarding the care of the minor children.

To create a valid Will, the document should be in writing. The testator or the maker of a Will and testament should be an adult with a sound mind. This means that the testator has the ability to understand every issue being address on the Will. The Will should be signed, and if the testator is unable to sign the document, he or she should assign another individual that can sign a Will on their behalf, provided that another witness is present. The signature of the third party should be notarized. A Will remain valid and can be enforced until it is revoked or becomes outdated by another Will.

Trusting a Trust in Estate Planning

Another Estate Planning tool is a Trust. Trusts may serve as a substitute or supplement for Wills. It also helps the testator to manage the property while he or she is alive.

This means that the testator can update or make changes on the property transition before death.

Creating a Trust

Creating your Trust is fairly simple. To draft this Estate Planning document, the property owner, who is called the "grantor" or "Trustor", must transfer the legal ownership of the estate to an institution or other person called a Trustee. The Trustee would be the one responsible in managing the property on behalf of the beneficiary. The beneficiary is the person who will receive the estate at the time of death of the Trustor.

Generally, a Trust creates a fiduciary relationship between Trustees up to the beneficiary. This means that the Trustee should act based on the best interests of the beneficiary when managing the property. If the Trustee fails to live up with this duty, he or she would be legally responsible for any damages. The Trustor can also name himself as the beneficiary of the Trust.

Types of Trusts

Trusts have two broad categories, living Trusts and testamentary Trusts. A testamentary Trust is a document that can transfer property into the Trusts upon the death of a grantor. It typically includes the provision of a Will, allowing the grantor to identify the conditions for receipt of benefits rather than making a single gift.

On the other hand, living Trusts are enforced during the life of the grantor. Living Trusts are designed to continue after the death of the grantor. It is a type of Trust that may prevent the document to undergo probate during the property transfers or distribution.

A living Trust is either revocable or irrevocable. Revocable living Trust can be amended or revoked by the grantor anytime after the Trusts were enforced. Revocable Trusts often act as a supplement for a Will. It may also serve as a legal document that permits the grantor to change the name of person who would manage the affairs in the event of the grantor's incapacity.

When it comes to irrevocable Trusts, the grantor can permanently give up his or her right to make changes in the document after the Trusts are created.

With regard to transferring assets, irrevocable Trusts can transfer assets prior to death and avoid the probate, an expensive and long process for transferring the estate to the beneficiaries. Despite this, many people use revocable Trusts to avoid probate. Transferring the assets to the revocable Trust means that the grantor do not own any asset upon death. People can only avoid probate successfully through revocable Trusts, provided that all the assets had been transferred to the Trusts while the grantor was still alive.

The Power of Power of Attorney

Estate Planning can also take care of financial and medical decision that is necessary upon a person's incapacity through power of attorney. Power attorney may fall into two categories; durable financial power of attorney or power of attorney for health care.

A durable financial power of attorney permits another individual to manage the financial affairs when the grantor is unable to make his or her own decision. Power of attorney can authorize another person to act on behalf of the grantor when it comes to financial issues, transactions and other affairs.

The person who will handle the financial affairs is called the attorney-in-fact. The attorney-in-fact may pay the medical expenses, manage the real estate property and transfer or sell the assets upon the grantor's incapacity.

The attorney-in-fact's legal authority over the financial affairs depends on the power specified in the document. Although the agent has a financial power, he or she must act in the best interest of the grantor.

Stop Procrastinating About Estate Planning:

A power of attorney takes into effect after the grantor signs it. If the power of attorney is durable, the authority given to the agent will always be there. If it is not durable, the power of the agent is limited. A non-durable power of attorney may authorize the agent, and that authority will be extinguished when the grantor is able to make financial decisions again.

The authority given by the financial power of attorney is automatically extinguished upon the death of the grantor. This means that the attorney-in-fact can act on behalf of the grantor while he or she is still alive or incapacitated. The power of attorney can also be extinguished if the name of the agent is not available, or if the court considered the document invalid.

Potential Medical Decisions

Making end-of-life decisions for the sake of another person can be very difficult. Choices regarding life support, hospital that would provide the treatment and consent on performing autopsy upon death, are among the issues involved in medical decisions. With Estate Planning, however, the choices and wishes of an individual regarding medical and end-of-life decisions can be arranged ahead of time.

Living Wills and power of attorney for health care may carry out end-of-life care choices and medical decisions.

These documents spare the loved ones from making difficult decisions for the sake of an incapacitated person.

A living Will is basically different from a typical Will that transfer assets. This document is designed to inform the loved ones about what kind of treatment that you want or do not want to receive if a person becomes incapacitated. People may use a living Will and specify the kind of medical procedures you prefer.

When it comes to power of attorney for health care, a person may assign an agent that will make medical decisions on their behalf. This document is essential if the certain medical decisions are not addressed in the living Will. The agent will carry out the wishes for the best interests of the grantor.

Living Wills and power of attorney for health care takes into effect when the doctor declares that the grantor lacks the ability to make medical decisions. An individual should be 18 and older to create a living Will or a power of attorney.

The authority given to agents through power of attorney ends when the grantor dies. This means that the agent only has the authority while the grantor is alive but incapacitated. The same goes with living Wills. A power of attorney of health care can be affected by a divorce, particularly if the person names his or her spouse as a healthcare agent in the Estate Planning document.

Celebrity Mistakes in Estate Planning

Considering the success of the rich and the famous people, together with the vast amount of properties they accumulated in their career, most people assumed that celebrities and high-profile people are familiar with Estate Planning because they have connections and does not have to worry about legal expenses. Familiarity in Estate Planning is sometimes not enough however. Planning for end-of-life and transferring of assets requires a thorough review and deliberation from an individual.

Despite the connections and accessibility of celebrities to Estate Planning help, some of them are guilty of committing the biggest Estate Planning mistakes. Such mistakes range from failure to update a Will to failing to sign the legal document up to not considering Estate Planning at all.

Fortunately, every mistake may provide valuable lessons for everyone. With regard to celebrities, their Estate Planning mistakes are a treasure that Will inform us about the "what-to-do" and "what-not-to-do" in creating an estate plan.

Chapter 2. Celebrities Who Were Not Able To Write A Will

Jimi Hendrix, Pablo Picasso, Sony Bono and Amy Winehouse all became successful in their career and unique endeavors. Besides being well-known celebrities, these famous individuals all have something in common, and that is not creating a Will when they died.

A Will is a common Estate Planning tool that specifies how the property and asset of an individual will be transferred to the rightful beneficiaries upon death. For some unknown reason, however, it seemed that Hendrix, Picasso, Bono and Winehouse never even considered Estate Planning in the first place.

Jimi Hendrix (November 27, 1942 – September 18, 1970)

Jimi Hendrix enjoyed his glory days as a music legend. When Hendrix died at the age of 27, it was confirmed that the music icon never left a Will though. Hendrix's estate was managed by an attorney for 20 years. Because no Will was created prior to his death, his family did not have the right to claim the assets and properties he left behind without taking the case in court. Hendrix's father, Al, filed a lawsuit over the rights to own his son's music.

Stop Procrastinating About Estate Planning:

Hendrix's father eventually won the battle and managed the estate until it grew to $80 million. When Hendrix's father died, his biological brother was not entitled to anything. Hendrix's estate was left to Al's adopted daughter from another marriage. Jimi Hendrix's brother claimed rights over the estate, citing that his father was manipulated by his adopted daughter in signing the Estate Planning documents. The judge later ruled that the estate should remain to the adopted daughter. Because of that verdict, Hendrix's brother never received a single penny from the music legend.

Lesson:

If Jimi Hendrix created a Will prior to his death, several portions of his estate would have been distributed to his close families, including his brother. With a Will, the conflicts between his father's adopted daughter to another marriage and biological brother could have been prevented. Without a Will, people who would never have been entitled to receive the estate Will in fact be granted a portion of the estate.

Pablo Picasso (October 25, 1881 – April 8, 1973)

Pablo Picasso is no different from Jimi Hendrix in that he failed to properly plan for his estate's division in death. Picasso was an iconic artist, accumulating estates that would be valued at more than $173 million today.

Despite his enormous fortune, Picasso's family never gained anything from those assets because the artist failed to consider Estate Planning. Apparently, when Picasso died in 1971, he failed to execute a Will. As a result, his estate was subject to taxes. To settle the tax bill, his paintings and other artwork were handed over to the Musee Picasso in Paris. A dispute also happened over Picasso's estate where his illegitimate son, and five other siblings, filed a lawsuit to claim the estate. The dispute lasted for years and ended after both parties reached a settlement.

Lesson:

Drafting a Will ahead of time may protect assets from estate taxes. A Will and testament also provide an individual the full control over how the financial affairs would be transferred to the family after he or she died. Without the document, the court will have the power to make the decision regarding the transferring of the assets. If that happens, the estate would be subject to huge loss because of the costly and complex probate process.

Sonny Bono (February 16, 1935 – January 5, 1998)

Sonny Bono's wife could have been spared from many legal battles if only the singer considered writing a Will. Unfortunately, Bono died in a skiing accident in 1998 before even drafting his last Will and testament. Because of this oversight, many people filed a lawsuit against Bono's estate, claiming a share of the estimated $1 million estate. According to a source, Bono's ex-wife, Cher sued for her share on the estate due to unpaid spousal support.

With Bono's Estate Planning mistake, his wife experienced a huge setback. Because of the non-existence of a Will, Bono's wife went through disputes and legal battles in court so she could be named as executor of her husband's estate.

Lesson:

If Sonny Bono had a Will that specified the beneficiaries of his estate when he died, his surviving spouse could have been spared from the stress and expenses of legal battles just to claim rights over her husband's assets. Lawsuits and other disputes filed against Bono's estate could have been prevented as well by having a well-drafted Will. Although there are certain laws that named an individual's spouse, the rules may vary greatly, particularly if the case involves divorce and remarriage.

Amy Winehouse (September 14, 1983-July 23, 2011)

Amy Winehouse was also found guilty of committing the number one Estate Planning mistake, not creating a Will. Winehouse was one of those music icons that died too soon. She died without leaving a Will that would have taken care of her estate. Many Estate Planning experts said that her career as a hard-living pop star prevented her from considering Estate Planning ahead of time. Being busy is not an excuse when it comes to Estate Planning however.

Reportedly, Amy Winehouse's estate is worth $4.7 million. A judge gave her estate to her parents, despite the fact that some of her friends believed that she would have wanted her ex-husband to get something from that estate.

Lesson:

Regardless of age or busy lifestyles, estate planning is significant. Creating a simple Will can identify how the assets will be transferred upon death. It may also ensure that the wishes of an individual will be carried out when he or she dies.

Steve McNair (February 14, 1973 – July 4, 2009)

People can die too young. No one can foresee a tragedy or the unexpected death of an individual, regardless if he or she is in the peak of a career. Even though dying too soon during your glory days is certainly heartbreaking, the loss can be more painful for the family if the person passes away without leaving a Will. One of those people is Steve Mcnair. McNair was at his peak of his career as a professional football player in the NFL when he died in 2009. Reportedly, Mcnair's girlfriend gunned him down, leaving his wife and children behind.

Because of Mcnair's lack of Estate Planning, his estate was submitted to probate court, which resulted in longer legal battles over the assets. The former NFL player's lack of planning led to further consequences as well. His mother was displaced from the 45-acre home, which McNair bought for her when he was still alive. His spouse needed to file a petition in a Tennessee court for more than three years to obtain $3.7 million of his estate. This portion was eventually used to pay the estate's back federal and state estate taxes.

Lesson:

Federal and state estate taxes are another important factor to consider in Estate Planning. Failure to plan may invite challenges to the estate, together with estate taxes and other disputes. Additionally, if the estate goes through the probate process, the estate will be vulnerable to losses and consequences.

Chapter 3. On Making The Necessary Updates To An Estate Plan

Simply having a Will or Trusts is not enough. Although drafting an Estate Planning document is one way to guarantee that the estate will be properly taken care of in the event of death, it is important to update document when significant life changes happen. If one of beneficiaries of the Trusts died unexpectedly, the estate plan should be amended. Different circumstances like birth of another baby, divorce and remarriage can greatly affect the estate plan. Unfortunately, a number of celebrities are not wise enough when it comes to maintaining their Wills or Trusts updated.

Michael Crichton (October 23 1942-November 4, 2008)

One of these celebrities is Michael Crichton. He was a best-selling author, physicbbian, director, screenwriter and producer. His famous works includes the medical fiction drama, ER and the box-office movie, Jurassic Park. Given the amount of assets he accumulated from writing best-selling novels and producing or directing fiction movies, most people assumed that he had a well-drafted estate plan in place.

When he died in 2008 due to a lymphoma, he had a Will that specifically excluded any unborn children as his heirs. This is a major setback to his unborn child because his wife was pregnant at the time of his death. This means that the children born after the Will was drafted would not get anything from their father's estate, simply because he failed to update his estate plan.

Although Crichton's estate plan would financially provide for his family members, including children and former spouses, his current wife was not named as a beneficiary. When Crichton died, the family had no time to grieve and immediately prepared for the legal battle over his estate.

According to sources, Sherri Alexander, Crichton's wife, filed a lawsuit seeking $7 million from her husband's estate. She contested that her $7 million share is included in the prenuptial agreement she signed with her husband in 2005 before they got married.

Aside from that, Taylor Crichton, the novelist's daughter counter-attacked Alexander's claim. She asked the court to remove Sherri as one of the three Trustees in Crichton's estate plan. The daughter claimed that Alexander breached her fiduciary duties as a Trustee. Sherri Alexander later pointed out that acting as a beneficiary and Trustee is not considered as breach of fiduciary duty. She stressed that the purpose of her petition was to include her son as an heir.

Stop Procrastinating About Estate Planning:

Lesson:

Crichton's Estate Planning mistake story may prove that failing to update an estate plan can lead to a contentious battle of families over the estate. If Crichton had updated his Will and Trusts at the time he learned that his wife is pregnant, any of the legal battle could have been avoided. It may also guarantee that his son would be well-provided for financially even after Crichton's death.

Heath Ledger (April 4, 1979 – January 22, 2008)

Heath Ledger also committed the common mistake of not updating an estate plan. Before his life ended, Ledger was an Australian actor, who is best known for his portrayals in several movies like Brokeback Mountain, The Imaginarium of Doctor Parnassus and The Dark Knight. The actor was aware of his success and guaranteed that his estate would be properly transferred to his beneficiaries when he died. He neglected to update his estate plan, however.

Ledger died unexpectedly in 2008 at a young age of 28. His estate plan was drafted three years before he died, the time when he was not married and did not have any children. According to his Will, all of his estate would be transferred to his parents and siblings, without any specifications about potential children in the future. Due to this, his daughter with actress Michelle Williams was cut out from the Will. Williams and Ledger developed a relationship not long after the Will was created. Because the actor failed to keep the estate plan updated, Matilda Rose, his daughter, would not get anything from his father. Ledger's relatives needed to fight later in court for the benefit of Matilda. Despite that, Ledger's Estate Planning mistake caused a very public and large family struggle.

Lesson:

When there are major life changes, the estate plan should also be amended. The estate plan should reflect the current situation and wishes of an individual. If Ledger updated his Will when his child was conceived, his wishes concerning the care for his daughter would have been carried out. Ledger's family could have avoided the stress of fighting in court for his daughter's rights and benefits of the estate.

Phillip Seymour Hoffman (July 23, 1967 – February 2, 2014)

The death of Philip Seymour Hoffman on February 2, 2014, was unexpected for everyone. Apparently, the Oscar-winning actor died of drug overdose. Hoffman reportedly drafted a Will that would provide for his family even after he was gone. Despite the existence of a Will,

Stop Procrastinating About Estate Planning:

the actor's estate plan became the victim of an Estate Planning mistake.

According to sources, Philip Hoffman's Will was accessible to the public because he only created a Will to secure his estate. He failed to consider drafting a revocable living Trust that could have been useful for his family.

Seymour had a significant amount of assets and properties, which was included in his Will before he died. To transfer the estate, the Will underwent a probate process. Probate court proceedings make an individual's estate plan a public record, allowing everyone to read the provisions of the Will. The procedure is necessary to read the entire Will. However, reviewing the Will in probate court can be an expensive and difficult process to deal with. The probate court is also the breeding ground for family fights.

Besides not creating revocable living Trusts, the Will that he created nine years ago was not updated when he died. In Estate Planning, failure to update an estate plan is a critical error. Due to this fact, his only benefited his oldest child, and not his two more children who were born after the Will was drafted. This means that the actor also failed to provide for his two daughters and named a guardian for them. His daughters may get their fair share of their father's estate based on the decision of the court.

Lesson:

With Estate Planning, parents can still provide for their family, especially to the children even after they died. However, there are parents, like Hoffman, who neglected to update their estate plan after drafting it. This critical error can cut out potential children in the future from their share of the estate. If that happens, the court gains control on how these children will obtain a fair share of the estate. Failure to update a Will also forces the estate plan to undergo the probate process, making the situation vulnerable to family conflicts and estate taxes.

Chapter 4. When Estate Taxes Attack the Estate Plan

Estate Planning experts do not encourage their clients to create an estate plan for nothing. They often suggest it so that their clients' assets are protected from financial implications that can greatly impact the estate and its potential beneficiaries. Estate Planning, however, does not mainly focus on asset transfers and fulfillment of the deceased's wishes, it should also consider estate taxes.

According to the IRS.gov, an estate tax is a tax imposed on an individual's right to transfer the property of another at the time of death. While this may sound easy, estate taxes may carry devastating consequences in Estate Planning. For one, estate taxes are different from probate expenses. Secondly, estate taxes, either imposed by the state or federal government, are expensive. A person obligated to pay estate taxes should pay in cash within nine months after death. This means that if the estate is subject to estate taxes, the beneficiaries of the estate will be the one responsible to pay the tax bill. Considering that some estates do not have enough cash, the estate usually undergoes liquidation to pay the bill.

However, the potential setbacks of estate taxes can be prevented by creating a thorough estate plan.

Unfortunately, some late celebrities seemed not aware of those strategies.

Elvis Presley (January 8, 1935-August 16, 1977)

Elvis Aaron Presley is among the music icons that influence the music of today. He is dubbed as "The King of Rock and Roll" or sometimes, "The King", amassing a vast amount of assets from shows records and even films. Despite his success and connections with Estate Planning attorneys and experts, Presley did not have an adequate estate plan when he died on August 16, 1977, at the age of 42.

Upon death, Presley's estate was roughly worth $10 million. Because of his fatal mistake of not creating an estate plan and considering probate, legal fees and estate taxes, his heirs suffered the further consequences. His estate underwent a probate court, making his Estate Planning documents became public. This also exposed his family to serious strain associated with court procedures. The King's estate was also attacked by estate taxes, slashing it by more than 70 percent of the estate. Because of this, the $10 million worth of assets that supposed to belong to his loved ones were reduced to only $3 million after estate taxes, legal expenses and probate expenses are taken out.

Lesson:

Stop Procrastinating About Estate Planning:

Simply devising an estate plan is not enough, given with the potential disadvantages associated with probate, legal fees and estate taxes. The devastating financial loss suffered by Elvis Presley's family could have been avoided if the "King of Rock and Roll" created an estate plan that can adequately transfer his assets to the heirs and save the assets from estate tax consequences at the same time.

Arthur Ochs "Punch" Sulzberger, Sr. – (February 5, 1926 –September 29, 2012)

Arthur Sulzberger, Sr. was an American businessman and well-known publisher of the New York Times. He became the publisher of the New York Times in 1963, at the aged of 37, making him the youngest publisher in the history at that time. Despite the rich information he acquired in different aspects of life due to the nature of his work, Sulzberger, Sr. is not different from the "King of Rock and Roll" with regard to Estate Planning.

Sulzberger's estate was reportedly worth $70.2 million when he died in 2012. The publisher left $41 million worth of the New York Times company stocks to his children. Unfortunately, the beneficiaries had to put these stocks into sale a few weeks later. The heirs decided to sell some of the stocks to pay the estate taxes. Because of the sale, the family's ownership of the New York Times was reduced to 13 percent. As of 2010, the Sulzberger's ownership of the publishing company had been 19 percent.

Lesson:

Families who have accumulated large assets are often the target of estate taxes. Because of the value of assets included in the estate, transferring it to the heirs and avoiding estate taxes requires a careful planning and consideration of certain circumstances. Although the government recently increased the estate tax exemption, it is critical for families who owned a large business to have an estate plan. Doing so may not only keep the business among the family members but also protect the surviving family from losses.

Edward Irving "Ed" Koch – (December 12, 1924- February 1, 2013)

Koch is known as the three-term mayor of New York, which basically increased his net worth. When he passed away on February 1, 2013, his assets were worth around $10 to $11 million, according to the documents in New York City's Surrogate's Court. Most of his wealth was obtained after he left the office in 1989.

Koch's managed to create an estate plan that will continuously provide for his favorite family members, his sister and her husband, sister-in-law and two children. His last Will and testament reported that his sister and

Stop Procrastinating About Estate Planning:

husband will receive $500,000, $50, 000 to his sister-in-law and $50,000 each for his two children. He also left $100,000 to his secretary and made a cash donation to a charity worth $100,000. His sister's three sons will also receive equal shares from his residuary estate. However, their inheritance will be lowered because of the estate taxes.

Koch evaded further tax consequences by leaving the residual estate to his nephews instead of his sister because there might have been additional taxes on the same assets in the event of his sister's death. Despite that, many Estate Planning experts believed that the estate taxes could have prevented if Koch leave the residue of his estate to a Trust.

Creating a Trust for the benefit of his nephews may protect the asset from creditors and former spouses. A $5.25 million worth of assets going to the Trust may exempt it by using the generation-skipping transfer tax. Generation-skipping transfer tax exemption may apply to grandchildren and remote descendants of the estate.

Besides these Estate Planning strategies, Koch could have lowered the estate taxes by taking advantage of deathbed gifts. When it comes to deathbed gifts, people can each give another individual of $14,000 per year without counting it against the $5.25 million allowable give way. Spouses can also use the annual estate tax exclusion, which is not only applicable upon death. Using the gift tax would have also saved his beneficiaries from an estimated amount of $600,000 in estate taxes.

Lesson:

Koch's Estate Planning mistake reminds people of the many lessons about estate taxes. The federal estate tax was imposed on estates that are worth more than $2 million. Although most people do not have the power to change the implementation of the federal estate tax law, there are Estate Planning techniques that can legally reduce the estate taxes upon death. Taking advantage of strategies and tax exemptions available in the given circumstance may save the heirs from the financial implications of estate tax bills. For this reason, it can be ensured that the family members and loved ones are well-taken care of upon their death.

William Davidson (December 5, 1922- March 13, 2009)

William Morse "Bill" Davidson was an American businessman known as an owner of the different sports franchise in the country. He was a President, Chairman and CEO of Guardian Industries, the leading worldwide manufacturer of automotive and architectural glass. He was also the chairman of Palace Sports Entertainment. Palace Sports Entertainment owned NBA's Detroit Pistons, WNBA's Detroit Shock and a co-owner of Detroit

Stop Procrastinating About Estate Planning:

Fury of the Arena Football League. Davidson also owned the Detroit Vipers of the IHL and Tampa Bay Lighting of the NHL. Forbes magazine ranked him as the 62nd richest man in the U.S. with $5.5 billion in net worth in 2008.

Considering the billions worth of assets at stake upon his death, Davidson prepared an estate plan that let him provide for his family even after he was gone. Unfortunately, he committed the critical error of taking estate taxes for granted.

When Davidson died on March 2009, most of his family members were surprised by the huge tax bill issued by the Internal Revenue Services. According to sources, Davidson's estate owed $2 billion in estate taxes to the IRS. Due to this, the business and sports franchise owner's estate invited many controversies and lawsuits to spare the estate from the huge loss.

In June 2013, Davidson's Estate Planning attorneys argued to the U.S. Tax Court regarding an IRS deficiency notice that inaccurately claimed $2.8 billion of estate taxes. The petition stressed that Davidson made transfers of Guardian's stocks to his children and grandchildren a few months before he passed away. The estate's lawyers contested that the IRS overvalued those stocks.

In contrast, the IRS countered that Davidson's estate and the gifts amounted to nearly $4.6 billion. The tax agency also discovered many deficiencies worth $900 million in gifts back in 2005 that subsequently created the tax bill.

Besides the IRS lawsuit, the estate conflicts resulted to family fights. Family members battled over the rights to control Davidson's charitable Trusts. Accordingly, a foundation was handed out with $46 million in grants in 2012, together with an additional $7.5 million for future giving. However, some relatives wanted to divide the foundation in two separate entities because Davidson's wife and two children did not have the ability to handle the foundation together.

Davidson also used self-cancelling installment notes. He used SCIN to sell the assets to his heirs who paid with promissory notes and required them to make payments while he was alive. The self-cancelling installment notes were eventually cancelled when Davidson died though. Cancelling the notes means the debt they owed to Davidson is also terminated and the assets would legally belong to them.

Although using a self-cancelling installment notes may avoid estate taxes, the IRS said that the payments of beneficiaries should have been higher. The assets qualified for taxes otherwise.

Stop Procrastinating About Estate Planning:

The IRS also challenged the tens of millions of dollars that Bill Davidson allocated to his wife. Although the IRS claimed that this is a gift, the businessman's estate disagreed. In the petition filed on August 14 2013, IRS emphasized that Davidson failed to properly account for huge gifts made to the family members and failed to list the accurate value of the stocks placed in a Trust for the beneficiaries. Because of this oversight, the more than $2 billion in estate taxes slammed against Davidson's estate was accurate.

Lesson:

It is critical for individuals to take federal estate taxes into account. With regard to Davidson's Estate Planning mistakes, he had the right intention to transfer his assets to his heirs through self-cancelling installation notes and charitable Trusts. However, the American businessman failed to properly make a correct accounting and valuation of some of the assets in his estate. An accounting error may be loopholes that can result in estate tax consequences after the IRS perform an audit.

Davidson also failed to specify his wishes because if he did, he could have prevented the fights between his families and other relatives. By creating an estate plan that will accurately and properly carry out the wishes of an individual upon death, potential arguments and dispute over the estate and control of the estate can be prevented, sparing the family from more controversy and emotional distress. Davidson could have use life insurance policies for the benefits of the heirs instead of self-cancelling installation notes.

Philip Seymour Hoffman (July 23, 1967 – February 2, 2014)

Philip Seymour Hoffman was famous for his award-moving movies like Capote, Charlie Wilson's War and Cold Mountain. His work in the entertainment industry helped him attain a vast amount of assets that would benefit the well-being of his family and children.

Unfortunately, Hoffman suddenly died on February 2, 2014 from a drug overdose. After his longtime partner filed a petition to open his estate and to probate his Will, many Estate Planning experts were not that happy in what they later found out.

According to sources, Hoffman is also one of those celebrities who committed critical errors in their estate plan. For one, he only used a last Will and testament to transfer his million dollars of the estate to his heirs. Relying solely on the Will is sometimes not advisable because it is vulnerable to probate, unlike Trusts. If a Will undergo the probate process, a portion of the estate would be taken out to settle the debts, taxes and legal fees. Probate also invites controversies and disputes

Stop Procrastinating About Estate Planning:

because it makes the estate plan accessible to the public.

Secondly, Hoffman created his Will with imagination, and with consideration to arts and culture. Many estate planners applauded the actor's creativity in including certain provisions in the Will that promote some of his beliefs, values and goals. Accordingly, Hoffman used his Will to express his wishes for his son. The Will stated that Cooper Hoffman would be raised in Manhattan, San Francisco and Chicago, or at least come to those cities twice a year, so that his child would be exposed to culture, architecture and arts of those cities.

However, Hoffman could do better than that. He could have put his assets in Trusts and place restrictions on how his children will obtain their inheritance. An individual may place certain conditions that should be met in order to distribute the assets from the Trusts. Setting up a separate Trust fund that will be used in helping his children expose to different cultures, architecture and arts in different cities might have been valuable as well.

Just like Heath Ledger, Hoffman failed to keep his Estate Planning documents updated. His Will was dated October 7, 2004, which is over nine years before he died. His Estate Planning mistake has a huge impact to his two more children because his Will only mentioned his son,

Cooper Hoffman. This means that his other children would not get anything from their father's asset without filing a petition on court.

Finally, Hoffman failed to consider estate taxes. The award-winning actor has an estimated wealth of $35 million. Due to the fact that he relied on will in transferring his estate to his beneficiaries, his estate was slammed with estate taxes. Reportedly, he left most of his assets to the mother of his children. Because Hoffman was never married to the mother, the entire assets are taxable. By doing the math and considering the current tax exemption and federal estate-tax exemption in New York State, Hoffman estate faces $15 million in estate taxes. There are also further tax consequences after the mother passed away.

Lesson:

Philip Seymour Hoffman could have been prevented the estate taxes issued against his assets. By properly devising a Trust that will hold the assets for the beneficiaries, Hoffman's families could have been spared from the costs, aggravations and delays in the probate court. They could have avoided the expensive legal fees and family fights and disputes over the estate. Probate process could have been prevented by simply creating revocable living Trusts.

Stop Procrastinating About Estate Planning:

With regard to estate taxes, people can lessen the tax bill by leaving the funds directly to a Trust. Marriage could have saved Hoffman's estate from $15 million in estate taxes because the assets can be transferred to his legal spouse for free. Marrying his long time partner may also avoid additional taxes after the mother passed away. Carefully considering the estate taxes could have allowed Hoffman to navigate different types of Trusts that can minimize the taxes.

Philip K. Wrigley – (December 5, 1894-April 12, 1977)

Back then, many prominent families own a business that remains in the family for generations. Such a company is often passed down to the child from their parents up to the next generation to come. For family members, their business is more than a property but a treasure they cannot let go. Keeping a family business upon the death of the owner may not be that complicated. However, if the owner fails to consider debts and estate taxes in their end-of-life decisions, their hard work and the great deal of time devoted for the business would be wasted.

Take, for example, the Estate Planning case of Philip K. Wrigley, an American businessman and an executive in the Major League Baseball. When he passed away in 1977, followed by his wife a few months later, their son William Wrigley became the heir to his estate. Wrigley's estate includes different sport franchise like the Chicago Cubs and Wrigley Field. Little did his son know, the wealth of his father from different businesses would be gone because of this Estate Planning mistake, failure to consider estate taxes in creating an estate plan.

According to sources, Wrigley's estate was slammed with nearly $40 million worth of estate taxes. To settle the tax bill, William Wrigley did not have a choice but to sold the blue-chip stocks of his father, which only amounted to about $13 million. The proceeds were not enough to pay the estate tax, forcing William to sell the Chicago Cubs for $20.5 million in 1981. As a result, the family's ownership of different businesses came to an end.

Lesson:

While the Wrigley family attorney stated that estate taxes ended the family ownership of the business, Estate Planning experts assured that there are other options that could have prevented the liquidation. If Philip K. Wrigley realizes the potential benefits of life insurance, his estate would be protected from estate taxes. Wrigley's case may illustrate that being wealthy and successful may come with a terrible price if an individual fails to take estate taxes into account. Lacks in-depth knowledge about thorough Estate Planning is a factor in many Estate Planning errors.

Chapter 5. When Estate Planning Goes Terribly Wrong

Sherman Helmsley (February 1, 1983 – July 24, 2012)

The American actor, Sherman Helmsley was well-known for his portrayal as George Jefferson in the television series "All in the Family" and "The Jefferson." Helmsley had an estate worth around $50,000 when he died in 2012 because of lung cancer. Not too long ago after the actor's death, a legal battle over his estate and wishes began.

According to the report, Helmsley named a "beloved partner" as the sole heir of his estate, as stated in the Will. However, a man from Philadelphia suddenly appeared and brought controversy regarding Helmsley's estate. Richard Thornton claimed that he was the actor's half-brother, which gave him the right to contest the Will if he and Helmsley are actually related. A test later proved that he is actually a blood relative of the deceased actor. For this reason, Thornton challenged the Will and demanded a share on the estate. Besides that, he also asked the court to let him take his brother's body back to Philadelphia, where the actor was born.

Thornton's demands resulted in an ugly court battle because Helmsley wished to be buried in El Paso, Texas, with military honors. Helmsley's half-brother contested the Will, arguing that the actor may not have been the one who drafted the Will because the document was signed six weeks before death. The woman named as the sole beneficiary of Helmsley's estate contested. She said that the actor never talked about his brother nor family before his death and she was the one who stayed by his side during those difficult times.

Thornton's demands and claims eventually delayed his half-brother's burial for months. It also forced the Will to undergo the probate court in order to settle the disputes while the actor's body was kept in a refrigerator for three and half months. Helmsley was finally laid to rest after a judge ruled that his half-brother can claim a share of the estate but carried out the actor's wish to be buried in El Paso, Texas.

Lesson:

Helmsley's Estate Planning case may emphasize the potential issues that may arise if a Will was created or signed several weeks before the person's death. Estate Planning experts confirmed that a Will signed close to death may imply that the Will and testament is invalid. Factors like the lack of capacity to sign a Will, signing a Will with unduly influence, fraud and failure to sign a Will in accordance with the state laws, may invalidate the legal document. Such factors are grounds for a Will contest and disputes over the estate.

Stop Procrastinating About Estate Planning:

However, family fights can be prevented through careful planning. A Will should be drafted not only for the proper disposition of the assets but to ensure that the wishes of the individual can be carried out upon death. An individual may also reinforce a provision that may prevent long lost relatives from contesting the Will.

Ted Williams (August 30, 1918 – July 5, 2002)

Helmsley's case may not be that different from Ted Williams, considering both celebrities could have saved their family from the chaos by drafting a proper Will. However, Williams' case is somewhat different due to lack of planning and the outcome of such error.

Ted Williams was a popular baseball athlete as a left fielder for the Boston Red Sox. During his professional career, he earned different titles like "Teddy Ballgame", "The Thumper, and "The Greatest Hitter Who Ever Lived." Unfortunately, Williams hit it low when he set up his estate plans.

Williams' Estate Planning mistake resulted in a dispute over what his family would do with his remains when he died in July 5, 2002 because of cardiac arrest. According to his Will, Williams desired to be cremated and his ashes be spread in the Florida Keys. However, William's youngest daughter and son chose to freeze his body cryogenically.

According to sources, Williams' together with his two sons and a daughter agreed to be put into biostasis after they die so that they can be together in the future. The baseball player's eldest daughter contested the said family agreement and filed a lawsuit to recognize her father's wishes in the Will. The lawsuit argued that the ink-stained napkin that indicated the family pact was null. She said that her two other siblings forged the note, alleging that the signature of their father was obtained illegally. However, a laboratory analysis confirmed that the signature found on the napkin was original.

Because of this, William's head was removed from his body and placed it in a container. His body was stored in another container. The cryogenic pact costs Williams' family of $120,000. The eldest daughter's lawsuit was later dropped. And because the legal fees from the court battle began to eat up the estate, they settled the issue by creating a Trust consisting the $645,000. The Trusts would be divided among the beneficiaries.

Reportedly, Williams' head was not that secured in the cryogenic storage. There were reports that claimed that his head had cracked and dropped, and suffered 10 deep fractures in the skull that have the same size of a dime. The Boston Red Sox's former baseball star's head is currently stored in a silver container labeled as ID number A-1949.

Stop Procrastinating About Estate Planning:

Lesson:

Disputes over the estate and the last wishes of an individual may arise if the document does not clearly indicate the desires of the person upon death. Ted William's case may illustrate the importance of creating an estate plan that specifically and clearly discusses the wishes regarding burial, transferring the assets and guardians of the minor children. After doing so, it is important to disclose the wishes to another person or a legal professional. The legal professional would serve as a witness, indicating that the wishes found in the document are valid.

Letting the family know about those wishes will be carried out is also essential. Doing so may let them understand that no one can act on their own or disregard your intentions in the Will. Williams' case can also illustrate that if the estate plan documents does not clearly specify what happens to the body, the next of kin will have the ability to make a decision regarding that matter.

Chapter 6. When There is An Estate Plan But it Lacks Adequate Planning

Will is a common Estate Planning tool for celebrities and even ordinary folks. Despite that, it is not the only Estate Planning option available at their disposal. Power of attorney is different from a Will but it can address end-of-life issues that cannot be discussed in a Will. The same goes with Trusts, which is a better way to transfer the assets to the heirs without worrying about probate or estate taxes.

James Gandolfini – (September 18, 1961-June 19, 2013)

Usually known as Tony Soprano, James Gandolfini is an award-winning American actor. He was praised for his character in different films and theatre. Despite his talents in acting, it seems that Gandolfini lacks proper planning in his estate plan.

When Gandolfini died in 2013 due to sudden heart attack, his estate was approximately worth $70 million, making his family excited for their possible inheritance. To dispose the assets to the beneficiaries, he created and signed a Will six months prior to his death. Unfortunately, he committed a critical error in his estate plan by only creating only one Estate Planning document.

Stop Procrastinating About Estate Planning:

Gandolfini set up a Trust, which was funded by the $7 million in life insurance. Because of this, his life insurance was spared from the estate taxes. The rest of his estate was not lucky though. Although 25 percent of his estate will go to his wife, the rest of his estate was not exempted from the $5.25 million estate tax exclusion in 2013. This means that some of his estate is subject to federal and state estate taxes. The estate would be 40 percent taxable, which may amount to $30 million of his $70 million estate.

Another issue in his Will is the inclusion a house that Gandolfini owned in Italy. Generally, properties located out of the U.S. cannot be included in a U.S. Will. To distribute a foreign asset, a foreign Will should be in place.

Gandolfini's lack of planning in his estate plan also showed when he stated that her daughter would get her inheritance when she turned 21. Estate Planning experts think that leaving millions of dollars to a 21-year-old can be inappropriate.

Lesson:

Gandolfini has good intentions when he created a Will. However, he should have been informed that leaving all the estate to a Will is a critical error because it automatically results in a probate process. He could have spared his family from all the legal troubles of probate proceedings by putting his estates into a Trust. When millions of dollars are at stake, revocable Trusts may prevent families from fighting over the estate because no one will know who gets what. Setting up Trusts may also reduce the estate tax consequences.

With regard to Gandolfini's foreign asset and property, a limited liability company may handle the matter. Setting up such kind of company may convert the foreign property into an intangible one, so it can be addressed in a U.S. Will. Another lesson would be that Gandolfini could have settled his daughter's inheritance by setting up a provision indicating that she can get the inheritance if she reaches a certain age and some conditions are met, such as graduation from college or earning a doctorate's degree.

Michael Jackson (August 29, 1958 – June 25, 2009)

The King of Pop had all the riches and fame. He was an American singer, actor, dancer and businessman. However, being rich and famous does not mean being smart and wise when it comes to Estate Planning. In fact, the "Billie Jean" singer committed several Estate Planning mistakes.

- Just like ordinary people, Jackson was a parent. However, he failed to protect his children's well-being in his estate plan. According to the report, when he died in 2009, Jackson failed to choose an appropriate guardian for his kids. The error happened when he chose his aging mother as the guardian of his children. Another uncertainty for the care of his children occurred when he named Diana Ross as a back-up guardian. He could have picked another person that is willing to accept the responsibility as the guardian of his children until they are adults in the event that his mother dies.

- Given with Michael Jackson's extreme popularity, he owned a vast amount of properties and assets. It had been found that these assets, ranging from investment accounts, bank accounts and insurance policies, are scattered. Because of this, his estate was subjected to probate court because of his unorganized financial accounts and record. This mistake reminds people that properly organizing financial records in Estate Planning is a must. Doing so may save family members from having a hard time accessing of all those accounts.

- He failed to anticipate estate taxes. While the "King of Pop" reportedly did a good job in choosing an unbiased person as the executor of his estate, he was not wise enough in taking estate taxes into account. Because of this, his estate would be paying high amount in estate taxes, which could have been avoided if he carefully plan his estate, established a life insurance policy and put it in a

Trust. The Trust may include his rights to the Beatles songs and gave it to his children in the future.

- Although Michael Jackson began his move in Estate Planning prior to his death, he reportedly failed to finish it. According to the report, Jackson created a Trust, but he never fully funded it. Because of this, the primary purpose of having a Trust was defeated. If he could have placed his assets into the Trust, his family did not have to fight in probate court over the

Chapter 7. Celebrity's Dumb Mistakes in Estate Planning

Warren Burger (September 17, 1907 – June 25, 1995)

Warren Burger was the former Chief Justice of the United States, dated from 1969-1986. Despite his familiarity with laws and different statutes, the 15th Chief Justice of the U.S. is same like everybody else when it comes to Estate Planning. Burger reportedly created a Will, but he did that on his own.

According to the report, a self-typed 1-page letter was the only document he left behind when he died in 1995. Writing a DIY Will may be inappropriate because it can automatically subject the estate to estate taxes. One rule in properly creating a Will is to draft it under the guidance or assistance of an Estate Planning professional. If Burger could have done that, his family did not have to pay $450,000 in estate taxes and had avoided the legal expenses to open his Will in probate court. The costs of probating the DIY Will could have been prevented if he had used a Trust or gifts to administer the assets to his loved ones.

Florence "Flo Jo" Griffith Joyner (December 21, 1959-September 21, 1998)

The talented American track and field athlete may have been busy with her trainings for her beloved sport. But that is not an excuse in committing a vital error in her Estate Planning. The Olympic sprinter reportedly made a Will. Unfortunately, no one, not even her family, knew where the document is. Due because her husband was unable to find the Will, he had to go to the court to fight her mother over his wife's wishes. Flojo's mother claimed that her daughter promised that she could stay in the marital home where her husband lives. To settle the athlete's estate, a judge appointed a third party to administer the estate.

Marlon Brando (April 3, 1924-July 1, 2004)

Everybody loves Marlon Brando. From his film and other movies, "Major Domo" is always a fan-favorite. Although the actor knew the way to people's hearts, he was not familiar enough with Estate Planning.

Reportedly, Brando made oral promises to his chief assistant and homemaker before he passed away in 2004. Borlaza claimed that the American actor promised to give her the Orange County home, beachfront Tahitian bungalow and she would always have a job in Brando's company. The homemaker was closed to Brando's family. She also assigned as the guardian of Brando's son.

In June 2004, Borlaza claimed that the codicil to Brando's Will was forged, alleging that he was too sick to have the ability to update his Will at the time. Because of this, the chief assistant was removed as the co-executor of Brando's $21.6 million estate. The dispute over Brando's estate ended after the family paid Borlaza of $125,000 in settlement.

Leona Helmsley (July 4, 1920 – August 20, 2007)

Leona Helmsley is an American businesswoman, known for her nicknamed as the "Queen of Mean". However, she is just like any ordinary folk who loves animals. The hotel tycoon loved her dog so much, so much that she left her pet with a vast amount of fortune when she died.

According to sources, her Will indicated that $5 billion of her estate would be placed on charity, while $7 billion would be left for his Maltese, named Trouble. Although she had two grandchildren, both of them were excluded from her Will. As a result, the grandchildren filed a petition to the estate, alleging that Helmsley was not in the right state of mind to establish a Will and a Trust before death. The plaintiffs won a settlement of $6 million while the toy dog's Trust was reduced to $2 million.

Marilyn Monroe (June 1, 1926 – August 5, 1962)

Marilyn Monroe was an American icon. She was popular for her motion pictures during the 1950s. Monroe was also an actress, model and singer, who became a major sex symbol ever since. It seemed that Monroe was so busy with her Hollywood life and failed to consider family relatives when she left most of her estate to her acting coach.

Americans are all shocked when they heard the sudden passing of Marilyn Monroe in 1962. Her fortune from her successful career was administered to her acting coach, Lee Stramburg. The acting coach reportedly received three-fourths of Monroe's estate. When Stramburg died, his third wife, who did not know Marilyn, claimed the estate. The woman hired a licensing company and auctioned most of Marilyn's belongings and sold the remaining estate to a branding company for nearly $30 million. Monroe's amazing legacy to the Americans could have been maintained if she set up a Trust that named someone willing to carry out her wishes and take care of her estate, instead of letting a complete stranger took it all and made such decision.

Doris Duke (November 22, 1912 – October 28, 1993)

Doris Duke may not be a model or an actress but she was certainly wealthy. Duke is an American heiress, the daughter of a wealthy tobacco tycoon. Because of her lifestyle, she trusted her butler so much, so much that she made him the executor of her estate. According to sources, when Duke died in 1993 at the age of 80, her butler was named as the executor and Trustee for a charitable foundation. With this, her butler would be responsible for the managing her $1.3 billion worth of the estate. However, the butler's questionable lifestyle and spending habits eventually removed him from the duty as an executor and Trustee of Duke's estate. A board of Trustee was later selected to settle the issue of managing the charitable foundation after the expensive legal battle over the estate, which cost big time to the charities.

Whitney Houston's Father

When Whitney Houston's father died, the singer was named as the beneficiary of his Will. This means that $1 million dollar payout would be given to Houston. However, her father's wife believed that Houston was not supposed to be the beneficiary of the estate. This sparked a legal battle between the daughter and the wife. The wife testified that Houston's dad took out the insurance policy to allow her singer daughter to pay off the mortgage loan that she applied to their own condo unit. Because there was no written agreement that support those claims, a judge eventually dismissed the case. The legal battle continued and finally ended in 2008.

Conclusion

Thank you again for downloading this book!

I hope this book was able to help you to understand more about Estate Planning, the brief preview in the life of celebrities who was guilty of committing different Estate Planning mistakes. With those mistakes, however, you are able to learn different lessons on what you need to do and what you need to avoid when you draft an estate plan.

The next step is to list the different Estate Planning lessons you learned in this book. Those lessons may remind you of why procrastinating is not advisable when it comes to Estate Planning.

Finally, if you enjoyed this book, please take the time to share your thoughts and post a review on Amazon. It'd be greatly appreciated!

Thank you and good luck!

www.ingramcontent.com/pod-product-compliance
Lightning Source LLC
Chambersburg PA
CBHW071814170526
45167CB00003B/1309